Simply Disconnected

Simon Gray was born in Hampshire and was educated at
Westminster School and in Canada and France before
reading English at Cambridge. His first play was produced
in 1967, since when he has had produced and published
more than thirty plays and a number of film screenplays;
he has also published four novels and three volumes of
diaries. His plays for the stage and television are published
by Faber in four volumes under the collective title *The
Definitive Simon Gray*.

SIMON GRAY

Simply Disconnected

faber and faber
LONDON · BOSTON

First published in 1996
by Faber and Faber Limited
3 Queen Square London WC1N 3AU

Photoset by Parker Typesetting Service, Leicester
Printed in England by Clays Ltd, St Ives plc

Simon Gray is hereby identified as author of this
work in accordance with Section 77 of the Copyright,
Designs and Patents Act 1988.

All rights whatsoever in this play are strictly reserved and
applications for permission to perform it, etc., must be made
in advance, before rehearsals begin, to Judy Daish Associates,
2 St Charles Place, London W10 6EG. No performance may be
given until a licence has been obtained.

A CIP record for this book
is available from the British Library
ISBN 0-571-17972-X

2 4 6 8 10 9 7 5 3 1

for Sarah

Simply Disconnected was first performed at the Minerva Theatre, Chichester, on 10 May 1996. The cast was as follows:

Simon Hench Alan Bates
Greg John Michie
Stephen Charles Kay
Jeff Gawn Grainger
Gwendoline Rosemary Martin
Julian Wood Benedick Bates
Mandy Nicola Duffett

Director Richard Wilson
Designer Julian McGowan
Lighting Designer Mick Hughes
Sound Designer Tom Lishman

Act One

Simon Hench's country house, down there – wherever that is. There are french windows stage right. A door to kitchen upstage right. A door off to hall, stage left. A drinks table, stage right. The room is comfortably furnished but slightly neglected. There is a CD apparatus. Slightly wilting flowers in a vase. Books on bookshelves, with an unread look to them. There is also a neat desk in a corner, a telephone on it. Several armchairs, as well as a straight-backed chair at the desk.

Simon is sitting stiffly in a corner of the sofa, arms folded. On the CD equipment, a church choir, amateurish and not expertly recorded, is playing. Simon's concentration is absolute, as if waiting for a particular passage. Nods his head, smiles occasionally.

There is a screech of tyres off, car door slamming.

Greg, in his late twenties/early thirties, enters through the french windows. He is wearing jeans, open-necked checked shirt, trainers. Slightly ill-kempt.

Greg The missus here?

Simon She was, I think. Heard her hoovering upstairs not long ago. She must have gone.

Greg She's not at home. And I didn't see her on the road. Oh, there she is. (*as duet begins on CD*) And there's your missus too.

Simon (*Gets up, goes to equipment.*) She has a lovely voice. Yours, I mean.

Greg Yours isn't bad. Flatter than mine, isn't she? Not

1

that I'm a judge.

Simon Together they make a beautiful (*turns off* CD) sound. Well matched.

Greg Well, where is she, my Mandy? I can't keep up with her. Even though she swore she'd be up here, doing your housework.

Simon Perhaps she went out through the front (*nodding to door, left*) while you were coming in by the back. You do have a habit of missing each other, I've noticed. Perhaps she's popped down to Mrs Camboy's for some shopping.

Greg Cambad's. It's Mrs Cambad's. Gertie Cambad's. All this time – what ten years down here, and you still can't get the name of the only shop right. (*Shakes his head.*)

Simon No, it's a problem I've always had. Even in my prime. With those closest to me. Very offensive, I'm told.

Greg What's the problem?

Simon One of identification, I assume.

Greg Well, your wife got the hang of us all in a few days. I remember as a boy, and she'd only been here for a few days, and she came up to me and asked, dunno what she asked, but she asked something. And remembered the answer, I'll bet.

Simon Well, I wish I'd got the hang of us. And you in particular, Greg. But nothing I can do about it at this stage of life, is there? So why don't you nip down to Mrs Camelwell's, boy's, bad's –

Greg Why? She'll come down the field, I'll go up the road, or we'll do it the other way round, just as you said, and there we'll be, missing each other again. Just as you said. Back where we started.

Simon Not quite. You'll be there and she'll be here. Different places.

Greg Best if I wait around until she comes back. That all right by you? (*Sits down impatiently.*)

Simon (*Looks towards CD.*) I was planning to go on listening to the choir. I tend to do that, at this hour, on a Sunday.

Greg Go ahead. I like it. Perhaps she's gone down to get our supper and a bottle for me. For the football later. Or she's – she's – (*Jogs his leg.*) doing something. (*Little pause.*) Go ahead. Don't mind me. But I can't help worrying. Worrying and fretting when she vanishes like this. And it always falls on me. The responsibility. And here I am, behind with the rent again. With all kinds of debts I probably don't even know about or can't remember.

Simon Ah, yes. The five hundred pounds, for instance. Which you borrowed to go to Antwerp. For a football match, wasn't it?

Greg It was Amsterdam. A cup final. I had to go.

Simon And the fine for hooliganism. And the ticket back again. Wasn't it five hundred?

Greg Something like that. That's what I mean. Debts just piling up all over the place. So where she is, where is she, is all I can think about, what's money compared to her safety – ah! (*In relief, as sound of car drawing up.*) You got a visitor, from the sound of it.

Car door slams, sound of feet on gravel.

Greg I'll be on my way. Leave you to it.

Stephen *enters through front, visibly shaken.*

3

Stephen Simon, there you are!

Simon Stephen, you're here. Why? Oh, this is Greg, Stephen. Stephen, my brother Greg. I mean, my brother Stephen.

Stephen Yes, hello, hello, can I use your phone please? I want the police.

Simon (*Gestures to it.*) Help yourself.

Stephen (*Picks it up, begins to dial.*) There's no dialling tone.

Simon No. That's right. I've had it disconnected.

Stephen (*Suddenly fixing Greg with a stare, puts down telephone.*) I believe we've already met.

Greg What? Where?

Stephen About a mile down the road. You drove me off it. That's why I want the police.

Greg I've never seen you before. Never. To my knowledge.

Stephen You came out of a side road. Completely ignored the stop sign. Cut right across my bonnet.

Greg (*bewildered*) Your bonnet?

Stephen Yes. My bonnet. At about seventy miles per hour, I clocked it at. If I'd been a fraction further on I'd be a dead man now. So would you. I was driving our Dormobile. A sixties Dormobile. Remember?

Greg A Dormobile from the sixties? (*Shakes his head.*) Didn't see anything like that. Can't have been me. (*Little pause.*) No way.

Stephen It was you all right. I'll never forget that face of yours. Grinning through the window. Shaking your fist. Were you drunk? Or what? Haven't you (*to Simon*) got a

4

phone that works? This is a police matter. It was *your* car. That Daimler of yours. Black. Do you let him drive it?

Simon He's my chauffeur, it's true. Not that I go anywhere –

Stephen Supposing I'd been a mother. In a car full of children. Suppose that, will you? And supposing you'd come across me in my other hat!

Greg (*bewildered*) Other hat?

Stephen I'm a magistrate. In North London. If you'd come before me I'd have thrown the book at you. Any magistrate would.

Greg Well, I don't know. Our lot down here are pretty fair.

Stephen What do you mean ? What the – the – do you mean?

Simon I think what Greg means is that down here he wouldn't come before a magistrate who'd be his one and only witness before throwing the book at the man he'd both accused and was trying. As well as sentencing. He'd get a colleague to do it for him. I think that's all Greg means.

Greg Yes, that's what I mean. Without having the words to say it. Now I'd better go looking for my Mandy. She's probably stopped off at the pub in case I'm there. Sorry about you and this Dormobile. (*To Stephen, hurries out.*)

> There is a pause.
> Sound of Greg screeching off.

Stephen Listen to him! Just listen to him! It's your car all right! Is he really the best you can do for a chauffeur, careless and homicidal – especially when you don't even need a chauffeur, you say.

Simon He happens to be living with Mandy. The girl who does my housework. So I had to find something for him to do.

Stephen Did you? Why?

Simon So that I could pay him.

Stephen Why? Why do you want to pay him, if all he does is drive about in a car you don't use, nearly killing people? Why, Simon?

Simon Because if I didn't pay him I wouldn't have been able to employ her. And Beth liked her. Took her on to dust, wash the floors, make the bed – whatever she does, when she's here.

Stephen When she's here! Another of your parasites, is she? Like that Dave you had lodging in your house in London years ago, the poly student who never sat a single exam, then moved his girlfriend in with you. And then she moved her ex-boyfriend in. Before you knew it your house was virtually taken over by layabouts. How Beth put up with it – ! Well, I must say, speaking as one who's sick to death of the Daves and the Gregs and – and what's-her-name –

Simon Mandy, her name is. She means a lot to me. I need her.

Stephen And overpay her. And employ her husband. How would you feel if he – because of your odd – odd – he caused a death on the road?

Simon My odd what, Stephen?

Stephen Your odd tolerance, Simon. That you seem to have been born with. I was thinking about it on the way down here. Remembering the moment, four years ago, wasn't it? – when you told me that Beth had finally –

finally – left. How calm, how relaxed you were.

Simon Left? Beth?

Stephen Beth. Yes. When she left.

Simon She didn't 'leave', Stephen. She died of a heart attack. In the middle of singing her duet. Up in the church. And I don't know how I seemed when I announced the fact. To you and others. But I trust I was seemly.

Stephen Oh, yes. You're always seemly. Whatever. Seemly and tolerant. Always.

Simon Surely you haven't driven all the way down here to have a row with me about my seemliness and tolerance. How's – how's – ?

Stephen Teresa.

Simon Everything all right at home?

Stephen Teresa's fine, thank you. Revelling in the grandchildren. The children are prospering too – Tom, Harry and Henrietta – in case you've forgotten. Henrietta's just served up another one for Teresa to babysit –

Simon And you yourself? Fiddle-fit, as you used to say. You certainly look fiddle-fit.

Stephen Yes, fiddle-fit, Simon, thanks. (*Little pause.*) A few problems at school, but I think they'll be sorted out in due course. Any minute now, in fact. Does it occur to you that there's another oddness? Asking how my family is, how I am, after all this time? I've written to you and written to you, made numerous phone calls to your disconnected telephone, and I haven't received as much as a card or a phone call back.

Simon But here you are. Wonderfully are.

Stephen Thanks to Teresa. She finally said, 'Why not go down and see him, just turn up!' Why did you cut off your phone?

Simon I didn't want to answer it.

Stephen Or answer my letters?

Simon I didn't open them.

Stephen Because of Beth? Is that why you've cut yourself off?

Simon What problems at school? That you think you've sorted out?

Stephen Oh, nothing. Nothing really. I was accused of abusing one of the boys. That's all.

Simon What sort of abuse?

Stephen Sexual abuse, naturally, these days. But there's nothing to it. If you'd had a connected phone or opened my letters, you'd know all about it. A trivial incident. Trivial. You know what really happened to you, Simon? That you can't face? Beth's miscarriage. Her baby by another man –

Simon Steve. As you're here, tell me about it. What are the facts? As that's why you're really here.

Stephen There aren't any facts. It's all gossip, speculation – the result of a thirteen year old's mischief-making. Toby. His name is Toby. Toby Winch.

Simon And what mischief did he make, this Toby Wench?

Stephen Winch. Winch. Not Wench. Winch. He reported me for putting my hand on his bottom. And for fondling him. What I can't bear is that he was one of my best students. The best I've ever had. I enjoyed, yes, enjoyed *and* admired his essays. His flights of fantasy were unusual. Exceptional. He has genius. That's my view. In spite of everything he's brought on me. Genius. As a publisher, an ex-publisher, you'd have appreciated him.

Simon As an ex-publisher, possibly. What happened between you and young – young – thirteen-year-old – ?

Stephen He won the Worthington.

Simon Really? Did he? And what is it? The Worthington?

Stephen It's the prize for the best essay of the year. The most prized prize in the school. He'd beaten boys from higher forms. Seventeen year olds even. I was so thrilled for him. And for myself, I admit. After all, I considered him my prodigy.

Simon Prodigy?

Stephen Yes, yes, not to boast, but I've always singled him out for special attention.

Simon Yes. But you mean protégé, don't you?

Stephen What did I say?

Simon Prodigy. Or progeny. I can't remember which. But it wasn't protégé.

Stephen What does it matter, what does it matter, progeny, prodigy, protégé? But that's you again, you all over, Simon, interrupting with an irrelevant question – do you want to hear my story, or don't you?

Simon Of course I do.

Stephen Where was I?

There is a pause.

Simon Your satisfaction at his winning the – (*forgets name*) most prized prize in the school.

9

Stephen When I heard the news I let out a whoop of – well, sheer joy. And naturally I went off to find him. Eventually I turned him up. In the changing room. Getting ready for the Junior Colts match. Such a fine young cricketer. A natural. Left-handed. He already had his box on when he saw me. Getting into his flannels. He gave me a grin – quite unembarrassed – triumphant, in fact. I put my arms around him. Of course I did. Said a few words. Very few.

Simon What words did you say? However few?

Stephen Oh, I don't know. Nothing you wouldn't expect under the circumstances – 'Wonderful, wonderful, you wonderful boy!' – that kind of thing. Gave him a pat – an admiring pat – on the bottom. And left. That was the whole thing. The whole incident.

Simon Were there any witnesses?

Stephen Only the other boys playing cricket. The two teams.

Simon So that would be – minus the star witness himself – twenty-one other witnesses. Plus the two twelfth men. The scorers –

Stephen What does it matter who saw me? I'm not ashamed of my emotions. Never have been. I've been embracing boys and patting their rumps since I started as a Junior Master for over – what is it? Heavens, yes – thirty years ago. And for nearly fifteen of those years I've been Assistant Headmaster. I've seen young man after young man come into the headmastership over my head. And now a young woman. That's the latest trend. A woman as a headmaster. She's in her early thirties, full of the latest sociological pitter-patter, but a witch-hunter at heart. Yes. A witch-hunter. And a fascist. That's what she is, at heart. But what I can't forgive, forget, is that little Toby told his parents, a morally fashionably young couple, just what you'd expect these days, and they went to Helena –

Simon That's your headmaster? Helena?

Stephen – who went to the Board of Governors. Who went all over the place. Everywhere. I can't bear to go into it. But the governors are taking it seriously. And why, Simon? I'll tell you why, Simon. So that they can cut down on my pension. Possibly deprive me of it altogether. So how will I end up? Without a job, a pension, or even a home – our house belongs to the school, remember? No, I'll end up in the filthy media – those newspapers, even the so-called respectable ones like *The Times* – we won't be able to get away from it, not Teresa, not Tom, not Harry, poor little Henrietta, and their children, my grandchildren. My face, my name, with those words they're so fond of these days – 'shamed', 'disgraced' assistant headmaster of famous public school! My whole working life, thirty years as Assistant Headmaster, twelve as a practising magistrate – ending in nationwide humiliation. 'Shamed', 'disgraced', homeless, penniless. And all because Toby, Toby of all my best boys – my very best boy –

Simon Have they reached their verdict yet? The governors? In a press release sort of way?

Stephen They convened an hour before I set off to come down here.

Simon Ah.

Stephen Ah! What do you mean, ah?

Simon Only that there's nothing you can do. Either of us can do. (*Little pause.*) The die is cast. Your fate is sealed. That's all I meant by 'Ah!'

Stephen And that's what you'll say at the end of it all, is it? Homeless, penniless, disgraced, shamed. A universal laughing stock. That's how you'll sum up your brother's life. With an 'Ah! Ah!'

Simon I could say, 'Woe! Woe! But whether 'Woe!' or 'Ah!' there's nothing we can do. The verdict will be the verdict. But as you're down here, who'll receive the news?

Stephen Teresa. One of the boys. Henrietta. Probably Teresa. I hope to God somebody's around to support her. I should phone, shouldn't I? To find out. What a coward I am! I've got to phone. (*Goes to telephone.*)

Simon It doesn't work, remember?

Stephen Oh, that's right. I'll stop at a station then. The first station –

Sound of car drawing up. Feet crunching across gravel.

Jeff (*off*) Simon – Simon are you there? Is this you?

Simon I think so, yes.

Jeff enters.

Jeff It *is* you. Tracked you down at last. I bring you greetings from the world you abandoned. (*Goes to Simon, embraces him.*) Years ago. Years and years. Christ, a lifetime it seems. How are you? How are you, how are you? (*Shaking him.*)

Simon Oh, I'm very, really – all things considered. You've met my brother, Stephen, haven't you? Stephen, you've met Jeff, I think. Jeff Golding. One of my oldest –

Jeff Oldest. And dearest. (*Takes in Stephen.*) Oh, yes. The school pederast. How do you do again? (*To Simon*) I've brought Gwendoline along. Never travel without her these days. She's whipped back to a garden shop she spotted down the road. Shouldn't be long as she's taken the car. She's dying to see you.

12

Stephen What – what did you call me?

Jeff Mmmm?

Stephen You called me the school pederast.

Jeff Isn't that how you introduced yourself, the first time we met? As the school pederast. At – at Amplebums or somewhere, you taught at, wasn't it?

Stephen Sides! Amplesides! Introduced myself – introduced myself as the school – the school – what the hell do you mean?

Jeff Well, nothing insulting, I promise. (*Looks towards Simon.*) You were there, weren't you, Simon? Of course you were, why else (*to Stephen*) would we have met? It was merely banter. A bit of banter. As I recall. You – let me think – you told me what you did, and I made some – some – this was back in the what? late sixties, early seventies – some smart-arsed remark about public schools and homosexuality, and you took it up – one thing led to another – I really don't know – but at our next meeting, that's it, our next and last meeting, you revived the whole thing by sarcastically introducing yourself, reminding me of our one previous meeting, you see, as 'the school pederast'. I've always remembered it. Don't know why. Part of the woof and weave, whatever the phrase is, the travesty – no, no, *tapestry* of human life. Human English life, anyway. Eh, Simon? In the middle classes, at least. As we were then. Twenty-five or so years ago.

Stephen So – so – you take it back then, do you?

Jeff Well, I can't take it back really, can I? As I never meant it in the first place. (*Looks at Simon in incredulity.*) I don't go around insulting people I don't give a damn about, you know. Not any more, anyway.

Simon Well then, that's all right, isn't it, Steve. An old

13

account accounted for.

Stephen Yes, yes. Apology accepted. All forgotten and – (*gestures*) congratulations, by the way. On your many successes since then. Teresa's a great fan. And my children. And even my grandchildren. Great fans.

Jeff Thank you. Thank you and thank them on my behalf. But doesn't it take you back. Just think. There I was, a half-baked flop of a literary reviewer sneering away at public schools as anachronisms. Except as nests for perverts. And now there you are, here you are – or are you still at Ample – Ample – (*Gestures.*)

Stephen Sides. Sides. Yes, I am.

Jeff Good for you. You stuck it out, and you've turned out to be absolutely right. Your lot are right back in the mainstream, politically and socially. Although I imagine the rules and codes, and so forth, are slightly different. Given today's moral climate. Which is strictly for imbeciles.

Stephen I couldn't agree more. For imbeciles. Strictly for imbeciles, our moral climate. But what can we do but change with the times. Adapt, adapt – that's our way. Always has been.

Jeff If I'd had a child I'd have sent him to you. Count on it.

Stephen Really? To Amplesides?

Jeff Well, not Amplesides because I've never really heard of it. But certainly Eton. Somewhere like that.

Stephen At Amplesides we pride ourselves on being superior in many respects – even to Eton – but I won't sell what doesn't need selling. Especially as you haven't got a son to sell it to. (*Laughs falsely.*) But I really must be on my way, Si. Long drive back. And a phone call to make. Above all, that phone call to make.

Simon I'm so sorry mine has stopped functioning.

Jeff Yes, the number of times I've tried to get through to you – (*to Stephen*) I've got a mobile, if that's any use? (*Taking it out of pocket.*)

Stephen No. No, thanks. I'm not quite ready yet to make the necessary – necessary contact. Well, nice to see you again. Everybody at home will be thrilled to hear that we've met again. Si, we'll be – be – (*Goes out.*)

Jeff (*Wags mobile in farewell as he punches buttons on it.*) Ah, hello darling, there you are, where are you? (*Listens.*) Blooming. Completely and utterly blooming, from the look of him, aren't you, Simon? Yes, yes, just like the flowers in your arms. Now hurry along and join us, bringing your own bloomers with you, of course. (*Listens, laughs filthily.*) Enough said. (*Turns off mobile, stands beaming at Simon.*)

Jeff She's on her way. Here in a minute.

Simon Good. Great. (*Gropes.*) Grand! But what about a drink?

Jeff Oh, no thanks. We don't touch the stuff any more. Though it's better if you don't offer her one.

Simon Right. But what are you doing down here, you and – and your Gwynith?

Jeff Gwendoline. Her name's Gwendoline.

Simon Ah! So you didn't marry your Welsh one?

Jeff What Welsh one?

Simon The Welsh one called Gwynith.

Jeff I've never in my life known a girl called Gwynith. And I'd never have dealings with a Welsh girl, whatever she looked like, think I'm mad?

Simon Sorry.

Jeff Don't be. I'm glad you've maintained your mastery of names. It's reassuring. It means you're still you.

Simon Thank you. And thank you for coming all the way down here to see me –

Jeff Well, to be honest, we haven't, quite. We were just passing through, the name of the village struck a chord, I asked about you at the pub – and here I am. Though actually, we're on our way to Plymouth. To do a book signing tomorrow morning.

Simon You've written a book then at last. That's marvellous, Jeff.

Jeff A book! I've written five of the buggers. No, six, counting this one. Don't you have a clue who I am these days, Simon? You heard your brother, didn't any of it register? I'm a bestseller. A household name. That's me.

Simon Well, I've been so out of touch down here, you see.

Jeff But I'm published by you! Don't you follow what goes on in your own old firm? Christ, your name is still attached. Huckle and Hench. If you took some shares when you sold out, I'll have made you a small fortune. While making myself a huge one.

Simon Well, thank you. What sort of books are they?

Jeff Travel books. With myself as comic hero. That's what turned the trick, my cottoning onto myself as sheer farce. So there I am, *Bungling Through Bombay, Toiling Around Turkey, Pootering Through Portugal* –

16

Simon Pottering that must be, mustn't it? Pottering through –

Jeff No, no, no. Pootering. Pootering. He's what gave me the impetus, re-reading his diary for a piece in one of the shittery reviews, dear old Pooter, my mentor, my golden goose, my inner doppelgänger – when I'm abroad I become him, you see – it's so bloody simple. I load myself up with compass, maps, binoculars, hire a bicycle – everything Pooter would do. They're sagas, you see, my books. Sagas of small catastrophes. I tumble into sewers, have rows in restaurants, mistake police cars for taxis – write up my diary every night. When I get home turn my diary into a book. On from there. Television rights, serial rights in dailies and Sundays, a film deal on the horizon –

Simon (*meditatively*) Actually. When you come to think of it –

Jeff What?

Simon Well, it's really rather brave of you. To make a living by courting misadventure.

Jeff Yes, it is. A risk a minute. But I enjoy it. And so do my fans. Like your brother and his family. They sit on their arses grinning and chortling their way through all my accidents and mishaps –

Sound of car drawing up. Car door opening, closing. Feet on gravel.

Jeff – and here she is. Speaking of fans. One of your biggest, Simon. Though I'm not sure you've ever met. But I've told her so much about you over the years –

Gwendoline enters. *She is carrying an enormous bouquet, seems slightly unsteady on her feet.*

Jeff Gwynith darling, here he really is. Just as I promised.

Simon, my wife Gwynith. Gwynith, my dearest and oldest Simon.

Gwendoline Who?

Jeff Simon. This is Simon, darling.

Gwendoline Yes, hello Simon, but who the hell (*to Jeff*) do you think I am?

Jeff What?

Gwendoline You just called me Gwynith. Who's Gwynith?

Jeff I don't know. I'm sorry, darling. A Welsh invention of Simon's –

Simon Yes, my fault, I'm afraid. I confused your name with one of Jeff's many old mistresses. Actually one who never existed in the first place. Being Welsh. (*Little pause.*) Or so Jeff tells me. (*Little pause.*) Have I got that right?

Jeff Yes, obviously I couldn't get Gwynith out of my head, once you'd planted the name, Simon. Much safer to stick to darling, eh, darling, whoever one's with – even a chap. Especially a chap. (*Laughs awkwardly.*) So. You OK, darling?

Gwendoline No, I'm not OK. Not at all OK, darling. I was just pulling out of the pub –

Jeff The pub? Why the pub, darling? You were going to the gardening centre –

Gwendoline But the best place to park, as it turned out, was outside the pub. (*Lurches slightly.*) I walked to the centre from there. Then walked back. Arms full of potted shrubs, these – (*shakes bouquet*) got into the car, backed out, just as some bloody fool in one of those antiques you can sleep the babies and the cats in – haven't seen one since I was a toddler, almost. (*Lurches again.*)

Jeff A Dormobile, you mean?

Simon Oh. My brother's got one of those. Stephen.

Gwendoline There was this face, snarling out of the window. Shaking his first. Honking his bloody horn. Complete lunatic. Missed my rear end by a whisker. Last thing you'd expect down here. A loony in a dormothing driving at twenty miles an hour and nearly killing you. I could be dead.

Jeff (*watching her closely*) Oh, darling, you haven't, have you?

Gwendoline (*Stumbles a little, backwards. Sits down on sofa.*) No, I mean it. (*To Simon, avoiding Jeff's scrutiny.*) Dead. (*Looks down at bouquet.*) Oh, this is for you. No, no, for your Beth. I wanted to put these on her grave, Sam. Or for you to, Sam.

Jeff Simon. He's Simon, darling.

Simon (*Takes flowers, bows slightly, puts them on table.*) That's very kind of you. I'll see that she gets them.

Jeff Oh Christ, forgive me, Simon. I meant to start with Beth. And apologize for not making the funeral. Actually, I didn't even know she was dead until I got it from Davina.

Gwendoline Davina? Who's Davina, darling?

Jeff Nobody, nobody. Just a piece of slag Simon and I knew once. Simon published a book of hers about some English colonialists in the Congo who stewed up a few Africans and ate them – something like that. *Boy's Own* stuff, really. She's clawed and fucked her way to the top though, head of series at the BBC, bought the rights of Bombay, Turkey and Samoa. So I have to see her from time to time. And what a sight she is! Fat. Well, portly, anyway. Spectacles hanging around her neck. Mole on her chin. Waddles. You'd be shocked, Simon – wouldn't recognize her even if she took her top off. Probably especially if she took her top off. But Christ, what tits she had! Those were the days, eh? All that passion spent. No, wasted. Sorry to cram all this in like this, Simon, dreadfully sorry about Beth, a great lady, one of my favourites, but darling (*he's been glancing apprehensively at her through speech, clearly not listening to himself*) we should be going, we've confirmed Simon's still alive. Time to move on. Plymouth calls. Where are the keys? I'll drive.

Gwendoline Took her top off for you, did she? No bra, I suppose.

Jeff Not then. Not that summer. The summer they stopped wearing them, which was the summer before they started burning them – you remember the summer, darling, you were around then after all, well Simon, thanks very much for letting us have a look at you – now darling, let's move arse.

Gwendoline I'd like a drink please, Sam.

Jeff Simon, his name's Simon, and darling if you don't mind –

Gwendoline Drink please, I said. Scotch. Another scotch, please.

Simon hesitates, glances at Jeff.

Gwendoline Now, please. Without furtive looks and glances –

Simon goes to drinks table, picks up malt whisky bottle, full, and glass.

Jeff You stopped off in the pub, on the way to the gardening centre, didn't you? Then stopped off again on the way back, didn't you? The pub. The bloody pub!

Simon (*handing over her drink*) There you are.

Gwendoline (*to Simon*) So what happened with the bare-boobed Davina, before she developed her wart and waddle?

Simon I've no idea. (*To Jeff*) What happened?

Jeff Christ, I don't know. Only what you told me. Or she told me. All I know is that it was at your place. I threw my drink over her and left, she took off her top because I'd soaked it, then strutted around negotiating a fuck or a book contract. Or both. According to you. Or according to her. Whichever one of you told me.

Gwendoline (*to Simon*) And how did the negotiations end?

Simon Well, I must have published the book. At least Jeff says I did. But then I published so many books without noticing them really, that I – cannibal stew in the Congo, was it, Jeff? (*Shakes his head.*) As for the rest of it – my place you say it happened. Then no. I don't think there would have been a fuck. Not in my place. Beth's and my place. Not our sort of style, really.

Jeff What does it matter whether there was a fuck, there have been millions since, this was all, Christ, a quarter of a century ago, when I was in my prime. Now darling, for the last time, can we please –

Gwendoline In your prime? You're always in your prime as a bloody fraud. A quarter of a century on from your prime as a drunken wreck of a fraud, you're in your prime again, and still a bloody fraud. Drunk or sober, a bloody fraud. That's you. Fraud, fraud, fraud!

Jeff (*after a pause*) We fought – we struggled and fought – to stop ourselves putting ourselves through this sort of thing ever again in our lives. We've done the lot, all the clinics from the Minnesota treatment in Arizona to Soaks in Surrey, AA, Promise, Protect, therapy here, therapy

there, therapy every fucking where, until we'd overcome –
until I thought we'd overcome at last.

Gwendoline Overcome? (*Laughs.*)

Jeff Yes. (*snarling*) Overcome.

Gwendoline holds out her glass for a refill. Simon refills.

Gwendoline Overcome what?

Jeff Overcome that! (*then bitingly*) Thanks, Simon.

Simon Not at all. But you, Jeff. What about you? (*offers bottle*)

Jeff (*glares at him*) What's the matter with you, Simon?
Don't you understand – ?

Gwendoline Haven't overcome *us*. *Us* is the problem, not
this. This – (*Raises glass to her lips, savouring the smell.
Gulps.*) is – oh, my God – bliss. That's what this is. But
why did I take up my bliss in the first place? I'll tell you
why. To keep up with him. He taught me about bliss in a
bottle. Then I had to give it up because he was going
sober, so he could Pooter, Pooter his way to a fortune. And
now I'm left behind in my bliss. All alone.

Jeff You're not all alone! You're bloody well not all alone!
However much I wish to Christ – ! (*Stops, brings himself
under control.*) Look darling, let's get in the car, open all
the windows, wing our way to Plymouth, they're
expecting us both. You as much as me.

Gwendoline They're expecting me to sit there maternally,
maternally watching you sign your fraudlings, your little
fraudlings, your babies, that's what he calls his fraudlings
of books, his babies. (*Laughs.*) 'With best wishes, Jeff
Golding' he writes all over his babies and they pay twelve,
thirteen quid – you know how he spawns these babies of
his? I'll tell you. (*Nods.*)

Jeff Remember this. This is something private. Secret. Just between the two of us. Remember that, Gwynith. (*Little pause.*) Before you speak another word, darling.

Gwendoline Like sex, eh? Except I'm not there to take part in it. Nor is Gwynith. Nor your topless from the seventies. Nobody but you. Wanking away into your computer. In your luxury suite. In the most luxurious hotel in the capital of the country you're pretending to visit. When he goes out it's on to his balcony. Then down to the restaurant for a gorge, back up to his luxury suite, consulting guide books, maps, making up his little comedies about himself wandering hopelessly through places he's never seen in his life, would rather be dead than have to cycle or walk to – fraud, fraud, fraud!

Jeff (*after a little pause, calm*) So what the hell. Simon knows that all biography is fiction, all fiction biography, and what does he care anyway, he doesn't read my books, he never read books even when he was publishing them, he just said so. So what the hell?

Gwendoline The hell for me is that we haven't fucked since you went sober to begin your first baby. Not a fuck in all these years, just your five babies. *Six* babies. Separate beds. Separate beds. Is the hell for me. Did you and your Beth have separate beds? (*To Simon*) Did you go on fucking, right to the end? Like man and wife – wife and man – did you?

Simon No. Though she did die in my arms, we weren't – (*gestures*)

Jeff How can you, how dare you – my oldest friend – he's my oldest and dearest and you reel in here and invade his past – well, that's enough. I apologize, Simon. From the bottom, the very bottom –

Gwendoline Nowhere else for you to apologize from. No

23

heart, no soul, all bottom.

Jeff I'm going. Are you coming or not?

Gwendoline Not. Bye-bye.

Jeff Can I have the car keys, please?

Gwendoline No.

Jeff Give me the keys!

Gwendoline (*Shakes her head.*) Go on, go and be a real explorer, fraud. Go and have lots of comic adventures on your way from down here to Portsmouth or wherever you're going, Pooter off and sign in a new baby – (*Waves him away, turns to Simon.*) She died in your arms. That's very moving. That's where people should die – not just in *your* arms, I mean, not all of us. But in somebody's.

> *Jeff lunges at her, tries to snatch the keys. There is a grotesque tussle, from which Jeff emerges, holding keys. Gwendoline picks up drink, throws it in Jeff's face. Jeff reels back slightly.*
> *Simon reaches into his pocket, takes out handkerchief, hands it to Jeff.*

Jeff (*wiping his face*) Thanks, Simon. Thanks. Always there when needed, eh? (*Makes to say something else, then puts his hand on Simon's shoulder, glances contemptuously at Gwendoline, goes out.*)

> *Sound of car door slamming, car driving off.*
> *There is a pause.*

Gwendoline Can I have another drink, please? I seem to have wasted the last one.

> *Simon pours her one.*

Gwendoline I'm dry. Completely dry. So I haven't got an excuse for taking my clothes off. Have I?

Simon (*thinks*) I'm sure you don't need an excuse. If you have a reason. (*Little pause, then as if discovering*) You know. I think the two may often be confused. Excuses and reasons.

Gwendoline And if I did take off my clothes, what would you do?

Simon Nothing.

Gwendoline Why not?

Simon I wouldn't have a reason for doing anything. Or even an excuse.

Gwendoline We'll see – see – if I can't give you an excuse. Or a reason even. (*Stands up, swaying.*) I've got good tits. *And* breasts. (*Fumbling at button on her blouse*) I've got a good body all around.

Simon Still – still – you'd do better – you really would – to keep it to yourself.

Gwendoline Why? Why? Because of your Beth? We'd be defiling your place together, her memory? Is that it?

Simon No. No, no, Gwy – Gwu – (*checks his confusion*) my dear. My wife no longer has a memory to defile. At least as far as I understand these things. It's *my* memory that would make me behave – um – discourteously.

Gwendoline I think I'm going to cry at last. Thank God. If I can't have a good fuck then a good cry – (*Sits staring at him. Doesn't cry.*) Can't. Can't do that either.

Simon I'm very sorry.

Gwendoline (*Gulps down drink.*) Well – I've had my bliss. That's it then. You want me to go, don't you?

Simon Not at all. Though I was wondering how you intended to proceed. To Penzance, I mean. For the book signing. Shall I call you a cab? There's bound to be a train for somewhere. From the nearest station. Which I think is – is (*points vaguely*) that way.

Gwendoline I don't need a train. All I have to do is totter down to the pub and there he'll be, toying with his soda water. Or diet Coke. Waiting for me. We'll scuffle about for a bit, he'll drag me to the car, open the windows, just as he said, and we'll be off to – to – it's Portsmouth, not Penzance. (*Little pause.*) Plymouth. For the baby signing. I love him, you know. Love him to bits.

Simon Yes. I've seen.

Gwendoline And he's the same. Loves *me* to bits.

Simon I've seen that too.

Gwendoline Sometimes in my sleep I try to kill myself. To get him over with.

Simon And yet (*taking her arm, guiding her to the french windows*) there he is. Down at the pub. Dieting off his Coke, waiting for you, not over with. I wish I could accompany you. But it seems to be one of those days. Who knows who else might turn up. I certainly don't. So I've got to stay here, haven't I? Oh, just a minute. You mustn't forget these. (*Gives her her bouquet with a little bow.*)

Gwendoline Thank you. Thank you, kind sir. (*Reels out.*)

> *Simon turns away.*
> *There is the screeching of tyres, slamming of car door.*
> *Greg enters. He is carrying two carrier bags.*

Simon Oh, not you. I've already had you, surely.

Greg Who was that?

Simon Mmmm?

Greg That stupid bitch. Looked pissed to me. Didn't

know where she was going. I nearly ran her over. Right there, on the drive. And she didn't even notice that she'd be dead if I hadn't – (*Makes dramatic steering wheel motions with carrier bags.*) Who was she?

Simon Just a passer-through. What can I do for you (*thinks*), Greg?

Greg What? Oh well, she wasn't up at the pub, my Mandy, I thought she might have come back down, but all there was was these (*indicating carrier bags*) and a note saying that the small package inside is your supper, and you've got to put the rest in your fridge because ours is defrosting, it's for her and me to get us through the next few days. (*Puts bags on floor.*) She wanted me to pay up, old Gertie Cambad did, but I explained it had to go on your account until I've sorted out who owes what –

Simon Greg, isn't there a matter of five hundred we haven't settled? Pounds I think –

Greg (*crashing in*) Where, where, where, that's what I want to know, where is she, what's she up to, is she seeing somebody, is that it? I've been driving around and around and what do I get, not a sight of her – and nothing to drink even, she always gets me a bottle when there's football, and there's football tonight, that's the one thing I've always counted on her for – a bottle of something for my football.

Simon picks up Gwendoline's malt, throws it casually to Greg, who catches it adroitly.

Greg (*Looks at it suspiciously.*) What is it? Oh, well, I suppose I can make do with it – but I tell you the picture of my Mandy trampling through some field or other, ending up in a ditch in the rain –

Simon But it's not raining. So at least it'll be a dry ditch –

Greg I could kill her! I can't go on like this – all this worrying and fretting, fretting and worrying, I can't, it isn't human, it isn't! But how do I stop myself? What do I do?

Simon Go back to the house. Once the football's on, put your feet up and glug happily away at your bottle – by the time you've finished it you won't notice whether she's there or not.

Greg Right! – If you say so, that's what I'll do. You're the boss man around here – (*Goes towards french windows.*) Oh, don't forget to put our stuff in your fridge, or she'll kill you, Mandy will. (*Goes out.*)

Simon looks at shopping bags, picks them up.
Voices off.

Greg (*reappears*) Somebody outside, asking for you – in here. (*Nodding to person off, goes, as:*)

Wood *enters. He is in his early thirties. Wears a run-down memory of a suit, Oxfamish. He is carrying two carrier bags.*
Off, sound of car door slamming, car starting up, off, as Simon and Wood size each other up, each holding their two carrier bags.

Wood Mr Hench?

Sound off, of car departing.

Simon Yes?

Wood I'm Wood. Julian Wood.

Simon starts slightly.

Wood Does the name mean anything to you?

Simon Wood? (*after a little pause*) How do you spell it?

Wood Usual way.

Simon That would be W-o-o-d, would it?

Wood Yes it would.

Simon Then no, it doesn't. The only Wood I knew was a long time ago, back when I was an undergraduate at Cambridge. But he spelt it V-u-l-d-t. He was German. Professor of Anglo-Saxon. Nothing memorable about him at all. Apart from the way he pronounced his name. As opposed to the way he spelt it.

Wood Nothing familiar about my face, either, eh?

Simon No. Should there be?

Wood Well, it's a matter of how you see faces. This face. That face. What's triggered off in you when you see them. (*Little pause.*) I'm here to enquire into your relationship with a seventeen-year-old woman called Joanna. You bumped into her briefly once, is my understanding.

Simon Really? When?

Wood Thirty-one years ago. To the day.

Simon (*laughs*) Really, young man! Do you think you can burst in here out of the blue, clutching a pair of carrier bags, (*suddenly aware of his own carrier bags, puts them down*) interrupting the meditations of my Sunday afternoon to ask me whether I can remember some – some – from thirty-one years ago? Really, young man!

Wood Is that your way of saying you do?

Simon No. It's my way of saying I don't.

Wood Just a minute. Just a minute. (*Puts down own carrier bags, fumbles through one of them.*) I've got something here that might help you. (*Takes out pistol, points it towards Simon.*)

Curtain.

Act Two

Curtain up on exactly same scene, Wood and Simon in exactly the same postures. There is a pause.

Simon Help? Help? (*looking at pistol*) In what respect, help?

Wood Help you to remember. Help you to answer a few of my questions.

Simon Fire away.

Wood Joanna. She was an art student, seventeen and living with an older man. Much older. His name was Strapley. You and Strapley knew each other from school. The famous public school you went to. Wundale. Does that ring any bells, Mr Hench? The name Strapley?

Simon Little bells perhaps. But little bells only. Very little ones. (*Pauses as he thinks.*) Strapley, Strapley – there's an association. Masturbation. Masturbation Strapley! I seem to recall a Masturbation Strapley. Though dimly. Is that who you mean?

Wood Except that he wasn't Masturbation Strapley. He was Wanker Strapley. But still, we're getting somewhere at last, aren't we?

Simon I hope so. (*Little pause.*) But where, exactly, are we getting?

Wood To a state of calm. Calm. How about you, Mr Hench?

Simon I was perfectly calm before we began our talk, thank you. Even calmer than I am now.

Wood Joanna. This Joanna of yours wanted to do pictures for books. She went around all the publishers with her port – her port – (*Wags gun in frustration.*)

Simon Folio. Portfolio.

Wood But I know where she ended up. That's the important part of it. In your office is where Joanna ended up. Stretched over your desk. Or on your couch. Or on your carpet. While you bumped into her, Mr Hench. Bumped and bumped. Into her. And Strapley, Wanker Strapley – Strapley, the Wundale Wanker – who'd left his wife, his two sons – Rhona, she was called, Rhona, never – now she never – (*stops, attempts to find words*) never 'recovered from the blow'. Those are the words. It was cancer that got her out of it. Yes, cancer. And two sons abandoned – two – two sons! – because of your Joanna. (*Stops.*) Because of her, this seventeen year old. Who wouldn't even marry him. So he changed his name to hers to make them respectable in the neighbourhood where he leased a flat for her. On her account. Threw his own name, his very identity, away on *her* account. And leased a flat on his account. On her account. So that's what he was, this Wanker. Wanker Strapley, the Wundale Wanker. Just somebody for you to laugh at, Mr Hench. Sad and lonely. A sad and lonely man abandoning everybody who loved him because of a seventeen-year-old art student called Joanna! While she was doing the rounds of the likes of you with her port – port –

Simon – fol – (*Stops himself.*)

Wood Yo – yo – yo, Mr Hench. Port – fol – ee – yo – yo-yo. Is that it? Portfolio?

Simon nods.

Wood Tracked her to your office. He knew at once what had happened. *You* had happened. Admitted it to him.

Yes. You admitted it to him, Mr Hench. No shame. No –
no – at what you'd done. Nothing. Perhaps you
apologized. Who knows? Do you know? Did you
apologize? When he went back to his flat. Her flat. In her
name. Paid for by him. What did he find? A message on
the answering machine. A message from Joanna, the
Joanna you'd just fucked on your sofa, your carpet, your
desk, the Joanna that he adored and you'd just fucked,
saying she'd never loved him, she'd only stayed with him
because she was sorry for him, because of the sacrifices
he'd made for her, the sacrifices of his wife, his two sons,
'hadn't known how to get out of it' was her phrase, 'out of
it', but now she'd fallen in love for the first time in her life,
fallen in love with you, Mr Hench, she understood –
understood what 'being in love was' – he listened to it
twenty times, fifty times, once. Once would be enough.
Because once he'd had enough of it he shot himself. With
this. (*Flourishes gun at Simon.*)

Simon I'm sorry. But if you can look at it from my point
of view – can you try to do that? And therefore logically. I
didn't kill your father. He killed himself. It was written
into his stars. He can't have been called (*slightest
hesitation*) the Wundale Wanker for nothing.

*Wood hurries to carrier bag, pulls out a pouch, shakes
powder onto his hand, snorts frantically, shudders in
painful ecstasy, relaxes visibly, blinks at Simon.*

Wood She left a diary, your Joanna. A diary and some
letters. I've got them here. You can have a little look. So
that you know what I know is true. Old man Hench.
(*Holds out a carrier bag, peers into it himself, changes it
for the other one, hands it to Simon.*)

*Simon pulls out a mass of pages – pages on pages –
envelopes, etcetera. He begins to read, with great
rapidity and expertise.*

Wood That's fast. Very fast, Simon.

Simon (*still reading*) Used to be an editor. Had to read everything at high speed. Before I became a commissioning editor. Then I didn't have to read anything. (*flicking through pages, concentrating*) I've retained the apprentice's knack. (*as an afterthought*) Julian.

Wood (*Watches Simon as he goes on flicking the pages, suddenly screams.*) That's enough, enough, you've seen enough to get the just of it.

Simon Gist of it. Yes, I have. (*putting pages back into carrier bag*) Julian.

Wood takes carrier bag from him. Puts it beside the other one. Sits down beside Simon.
Simon is staring into a kind of vacancy.

Wood Well, Simon?

There is a little pause.

Wood Well? Simon?

Simon A friend of mine, a very old friend, apparently my oldest friend, was saying just before you arrived that 'all biography is fiction. All fiction biography.' Julian.

Wood lets out a cry of pain.
Simon looks at him.

Wood (*muttering*) You'd better stop it with the Julians. I can't stand any more of your Julians. Makes me sound like your – your houseboy. Julian. (*Shouts.*) It's all true! You know it's all true! And the letters – the letters –

Simon I didn't read the letters. I assumed they were confi – (*reaching into bag*)

Wood Leave them! Leave them alone! (*Struggles with himself, then more calmly*) One of the letters is written by

33

you. Is that confi – confi – confi – to yourself? Or you didn't have to read it, because you remembered – eh, Hench? Mr Hench?

Simon I didn't recognize my handwriting on any of the envelopes. Most of the handwriting is flowery, affected, art-schooly –

Wood Her letters. Your Joanna's letters, you mean.

Simon She wasn't my Joanna. She's not there for me. And your wagging gun, your stuffing stuff up your nose, her diaries and letters, won't make her there for me. So, Mr Wood – Mr Strapley to give you the name you belong to, you might as well shoot me. Or go. Or both. You won't change my memory, whatever you do.

Wood gobs, makes to spit gob into Simon's face, checks himself, swallows.

Wood You'd make a very civilized corpse, that's what you're thinking. I'd make sure you wouldn't look civilized. You'd be all over the place. This part of you (*taps his skull with gun*) just like him, you'd look. Nobody could tell that part of you apart from that part of him. (*Gets up, walks around.*) Those letters she wrote to you, with the handwriting on the envelope, flowery, art-schooly, what was the other word?

Simon Affected, I think.

Wood You only opened the first one. The rest were returned – 'return to sender'. Unopened. Only the first one opened. And answered with a brief – a brief – (*thinks*) note from you. Ordering her to stop pestering you. What had happened on your desk, your sofa, your carpet, wherever it had happened, that was over. That was finis. Finis. Finis. The word. Finis. You enclosed a cheque for fifty pounds. 'This correspondence must close with the enclosed' you wrote, didn't you? Finis, finis, finished, you wrote.

Simon Did I? If I did I was quite right. One always ends up paying for these things. Best to accept that and – (*little pause*) pay up. Those were different times, Jul – (*stops himself*) Mr Wood. Or Strapley. As you prefer. You must understand that those were different times. A different age. Sex happened when the mood took one. Only VD to worry about. And there were pills for that. (*Little pause.*) Before your time. Long before your time.

Wood Not long before my time. The beginning of my time, is what it was. (*Begins to hum what becomes shortly 'Institutional Baby', stops.*) You didn't even bother to read her first letter, did you? You – you simply – scribbled out a cheque. For fifty pounds. Put your name to it. Finis. All over. Finished. Finis.

Simon I wonder if you'll understand this. Try and understand this. Sometimes, one used to find that an encounter that had been casually undertaken – as with this young art student – casually undertaken and satisfactorily concluded – (*gestures*) mutually casual, mutually concluded on one side, *my* side, wasn't thought to be concluded, wasn't thought to be casual or mutual, on the other side. *Her* side. (*Little pause.*) There were a few young women about, you see, who appeared to be the very embodiment of the times who turned out not to be in the *spirit* of the times. They had, poor souls, old-fashioned hearts. Young bodies. Strong desires. Old-fashioned hearts. She must have been one of those. In the world. Not of it.

Wood So you just cut her out. That was your system, was it?

Simon Much kinder than tears, explanations,

recriminations – surely, Julian, you understand that much?

Wood Kinder to yourself at least. I understand that much,
Mr – Mr –

Simon Simon.

Wood Hench. Mr Hench. And so the fifty pounds was a –
a – what was it, Mr Hench?

Simon A generous solution to a difficult case, Julian. After
all, fifty pounds was quite a sum in those days.

Wood So. (*Little pause*) That was the end of it for you,
was it, Si? Fin – fin – the end? A fuck followed by an
insult. You never thought, not for a second thought,
there'd be further con – con – con – the word. What's the
word?

Simon (*thinks*) Consequences. Could it be consequences,
Julian?

Wood Like my – myself, Hench. Mr Hench. Simon. My
father. I'm the con – con – con –

Simon (*automatically, dully*) – sequence. You're *my* son
then? Not Strapley's? Wanker Strapley's? Is that it? Your
story? What it amounts to?

Wood (*nods*) Yes, your son. Not the Wundale Wanker's.
(*Laughs.*) Yours. Finis. Finished. Because of you, because of
you and her I've spent time, all my time, in instit – instit –

> Simon makes to speak.
> Wood halts him with gun.

Wood – tutions. Institutions. Prisons. Yes. Mental bins.
Yes. I wrote a song. 'Institutional baby.' (*Begins to sing.*)
'Here I am/ Institutional baby/ Mama Jo/ Find a home/ For
your in-stit-ution-al baby.' She put me in an orphanage,
your one-fuck Joanna. Took me back. Got me into care.

36

Got me back. Here's another one. Listen to this. My 'Yo-Yo Boy.' (*Croons screechingly.*) 'Yo-Yo boy. Yo-Yo Boy/ Just another Yo-Yo? Portofol – ee – yo – Boy – y – y– y.' And here's another one – (*points the gun at Simon to shoot him*) 'Goodbye Daddy, So Long Daddy – here's the end – here's the end for Daddy – '

> *Simon folds his arms, hands beneath his armpits, waiting for shot.*
> *Sound of car drawing up. Door slamming. Footsteps on gravel.*
> *Wood folds his arms concealing gun underneath armpit as:*
> *Stephen enters.*

Stephen Simon! (*Stops, seeing Simon, Wood, facing each other, arms folded, in identical postures.*) Oh, sorry, I didn't know you had a guest.

Simon That's all right, Steve. You're not interrupting anything of – of consequence.

Wood I'd better be going. On my way.

Stephen (*looking at the two figures, in identical postures, to Wood*) Don't I know you? You remind me of somebody – I know! From school! Strapley! Can that be – are you related by any – Wanker of Wundale – (*laughs*) sorry. Sorry. But if you are related by any –

Wood (*cutting across him, to Simon*) Thank you very much for your time. (*Shaking slightly, goes to Simon's carrier bags, slips gun in, picks them up.*) And for your help – all your help – (*Walks to the door, then runs out, full tilt.*)

Stephen Well, then, who was he?

Simon Oh, just an itinerant. Asking for directions.

Stephen Where to?

Simon I don't know. I don't think he knew either. The world being so vague and chaotic – but what brings you back, Steve? I thought you'd gone. Weren't you – (*thinks*) on your way home? To bad news. Or – or –

Stephen (*laughs jubilantly*) That's what I thought too. But nothing could be further from the case. I stopped at the first service station to make that phone – call – no, not *that* one, to the school. I told myself not to be a coward, and phoned Teresa. Took the bull by the horns, in fact.

Simon And?

Stephen The police have decided not to press charges!

Simon The police? Really? I didn't know the police –

Stephen No, no, perhaps I didn't mention the police aspect. More than I could face mentioning, even to you, Si. But anyway, now I'm in the clear, I don't mind facing up to it. I could have gone to jail, you see.

Simon Well, that's certainly something to celebrate.

Stephen The rest is really just icing on the cake. I'm not being sacked, with dishonour. I'm being pensioned off.

Simon Oh, good!

Stephen True, I'm not getting my full pension. But we can stay in the house until the end of next term – that's three months, which will give us time to look around. Adjust to circumstances. What's a bit of belt-tightening compared to the prospect I was facing an hour or so ago? And there are the children, Harry, Tom, Henrietta – the grandchildren too, to revel in. Not a cloud in the sky. Except penury. (*Laughs.*)

Simon (*after a pause*) How many miles did you drive? Before driving back again?

Stephen Why?

Simon Don't know, really. Just wondering. Trying to imagine your – your journey. So – so fraught with anxiety – how far did you get?

Stephen But I've told you. To the first service station. The first telephone.

Simon Ah! (*nods*)

   There is a pause.

Stephen Ah? You're not in the slightest bit interested, are you? I've come all the way back to share the best news of my life, and you – you couldn't care less, could you?

Simon Of course I could. I could certainly care less, Steve. Really.

Stephen If you cared less, you'd be wishing me positive harm. Yes, you would. Well, here's something else you should know. About you and your fashionable, successful, smirking friends. I saw him on the road. Coming towards me.

Simon Which one?

Stephen The one I just met again. The famous writer. Here. In this very room. His car was swerving all over the place, he had some woman with him. I just managed to swing around him. Thank God nothing was coming in the opposite direction, or I'd be a – a –

Simon Pensionless goner.

Stephen What?

Simon Who was driving, did you notice? He or some woman?

Stephen What does it matter? Why did I do it? Why did I bother to come back?

Simon I don't know. Why did you?

Stephen I don't know either. Because you're my brother. The brother I never had.

Simon And you don't know who was driving, Jeff or some woman –

Stephen To hell with you, Si. To hell with you at last.

Simon That would seem an appropriate place to –

Stephen turns, exits.

Greg (*Simultaneously enters, looks over his shoulder.*) What's the matter with him this time? Nearly trampled all over me.

Simon (*Fixes Greg with a glassy smile.*) Greg, isn't it?

Greg What do you mean, Greg isn't it? 'Course it's Greg!

Simon Well then, Greg, what do you want?

Greg Our nosh is what I want.

Simon The football's over, the bottle finished – ?

Greg (*shaking his head*) Fuck the football. She could get home any moment, she'll be hungry – she needs her food more than ever, you know that – (*sees carrier bags*) not in the fridge, you didn't put them in the fridge, then? (*Picks up carrier bags.*)

Simon No. I'm sorry. I've had a stream of visitors –

Greg (*Peers into carrier bags.*) They'll be melting away – what's this? (*Takes out Wood's gun, bits of diary.*) And this, what's this? (*Takes out Wood's heroin kit from other bag.*) What's all this then?

Simon His paraphernalia.

Greg What? Who's what?

Simon Listen – (*gestures*) listen – um –

Greg Greg. Greg's the name. Greg.

Simon Yes. Listen, Greg. All that has nothing to do with you. They're his.

Greg Whose?

Simon His. I've told you.

Greg I could go to the police with this lot. (*Drops carrier bags contemptuously.*) But they'd probably blame me for these, that's the way they are, the police. And you'd back them up – that's your type, your – your style! Pig! (*Exits.*)

Stephen (*Enters, looking over his shoulder.*) What a rude, aggressive young thug of a man he is, he virtually pushed me out of his way. But that's what comes out of your household these days, Simon, isn't it? Rabble.

Simon So you're back already. Before you've left really, um – I noticed I didn't hear your car –

Stephen I've been sitting in it. Thinking. Thinking, thinking, thinking.

Simon (*after a little pause*) Have you? What about?

Stephen Oh, you mainly, I suppose, Simon.

Simon Then I'm very flattered. Given all your many problems – that you should spare a thought –

Stephen They were both driving.

Simon What?

Stephen Your fashionable friends. That's all you were interested in when I came in here a few minutes ago, teeming with good news about my future – all you wanted to know. Which of them was driving. Well, they both were. They were grappling with the steering wheel – death

41

on the road if ever I saw it. Your friends, Simon. Just like that young man – your employee, Simon – who nearly knocked me over. Doesn't Teresa mean anything to you? My children, your nephews and niece. My grandchildren, your – your –

Simon Great nephews and nieces, they'd be, wouldn't they? Or grand. One or the other. Great or grand.

Stephen Well? Do they or don't they?

Simon (*thinks*) What should they mean?

Stephen That's not for me to say. It's for you to say.

Simon I don't really know what they mean, um – Steve. If they have a meaning it's (*gestures*) escaped me. People are. If you see. Rather than mean. If you follow. However related they might – might –

Stephen Do you know what Beth said, just before she was taken? Sorry! *Died.*

Simon Yes. I was there. So I know exactly what she said. And as we were alone, she and I, you weren't there. So you haven't the slightest idea what she said. And I don't want to hear anything she might have –

Stephen She said – what she said to Teresa – she said, a month before we knew –

Simon Steve!

Stephen – any of us knew that she was ill. She said –

Simon I don't want to hear, Steve. I – don't – want – to – hear!

Stephen She said she wished she'd had that baby. Even if it was by another man. A man into whose arms you drove her. With your casual infidelities, your cool, predictable rationality. Your deadness of spirit. 'Yes,' she said, 'Yes. If you'd been a father, even if it wasn't your own child you were father of, you might have learnt how to live a life.' So what a tragedy – a tragedy that she lost it.

Simon She didn't 'lose' it. It died. As it was being born it died.

Stephen You've never given a thought, have you, to what you've done to other people? People who loved and needed you. Not least your Beth, whom we all loved and –

Simon Enough! That's enough, Stephen. Enough talk of babies, children, lives, unwanted deaths, unwanted lives – your mess is your mess, your muddle yours. It's nothing to do with me whether you molested a boy in the changing rooms, whether you're up before a beak, you're only my brother by some unnatural law of nature, beyond the comprehension of both of us. Go, please. Please go.

Stephen (*incredulously, after a pause*) You're throwing me out?

Simon No. No, of course not. I'm merely asking you to leave. Forthwith.

Stephen Very well. I'll go. Forthwith. Forth – I'll go. With.

Simon (*generously*) Thank you, Stephen. Thank you.

Stephen But don't expect me to forget this. Or forgive it. This is the end between us – between you and Teresa, between you and Harry, Tom, Henrietta and their children –

Simon (*Moans, in a kind of relief.*) Yes. If you say so. The end. Thank you.

Stephen You – you deserve everything you get.

Simon Everything I deserve, I've got.

Stephen Good! Good! I'm glad to hear it! To think I once called you brother! (*Goes out as:*)

Mandy *enters, heavily pregnant.*

Mandy Yo-ho (*dully*) motherfucker.

Simon (*suddenly alive*) Yo-ho, Mandy. You're not in a ditch, then? Not that I thought you were of course.

Mandy What ditch would I be in? Spent the whole day avoiding him as he went speeding round corners in that car of yours. Swarming into the pub, the shop, picking up meals. So yo. So ho. Motherfucker. Don't know where he is. Looking for me is where he is.

Simon I gather he's up at your house. Watching the football. So I gather – (*Pause.*) You still haven't told him?

Mandy Told him what? That you used to grab me and have me while I was down on my knees swabbing your hall floor?

Simon Yes, I know. I'm sorry. I was in love with you and therefore a little – shy, you see. I didn't know how else to go about it. In the old days I would have found a different – more graceful – method, I'm sure. At least I hope so.

Mandy And now I've got a baby that could be his, could be yours. Is that what you want me to tell him, old man?

Simon Yes, tell him. I don't care whether it's mine or his. Then you come here. Live with me.

Mandy No thanks. I've made up my mind. I'm staying down there with Greg. Where I belong.

Simon Why? What is he, that I'm not?

Mandy He is. That's what he is. And you're not.

Simon I'll try, Mandy. I'll really try.

Mandy That's not enough. Trying. You don't *be*. No, you don't. You just don't *be*!

Simon (*both calmly and desperately*) I need you both. You and the baby – you're all I've got. To the end of my life.

Mandy The end of your life, that's your business. You had your missus. She was a good lady, from what I could see of her. And hear of her. I liked our duets together, even if she was a bit flat from time to time and set my teeth grating. But you didn't love her from what I could see or hear of the two of you. Or if you did you didn't make much show of it. That's not for me.

Simon Let me have him. Or her. Whatever it is. I'm not particular. I'll take you both. Or all three. If they're twins. As you sometimes say they are. I'll give you all a good home – (*Gestures around.*)

Mandy You're proposing to me, is that what this is?

Simon I'm certainly making a proposal, from the sound of me.

> *Sound of car screeching up, car door slamming, footsteps angrily crunching. Greg enters.*

Greg Not a sign of her, not a (*sees Mandy*) – oh, so there you are then, I might have known I'd find you when I didn't expect you, all over the place I've been.

Mandy So what about you and your football?

Greg How could I look at football when it's you I'm after. Well, come on, then – and I've got myself a bottle, which is more than you did for me.

Mandy Go and get our supper from the fridge then and let's be gone from here.

Greg It's not there. (*Gestures to Wood's carrier bags.*)

This is what we got instead. A gun and lots of rubbish –

Simon Greg, there's something you should know.

Mandy No, there isn't, no, there isn't, there's nothing he should know.

Simon It's a business transaction, Mandy. Strictly between Greg and myself. It needn't concern you. That five hundred pounds we were discussing –

Greg I told you – I told you I'd pay you back when – when –

Simon No, it's another five hundred pounds. I want to – to contribute it to your family. Imminent family. Every month.

Greg gapes.

Simon All you have to do in return is let me babysit. Preferably on a regular basis. I've suddenly discovered, you see, rather late, that I'm – um – rather fond of children after all.

Greg Five hundred pounds! To be let babysit! Is that the deal?

Mandy No deal, Greg, there's no deal. Our babe's not for letting. Or hiring out. We don't take any money from him except what we earn. You understand that, Greg? Or I'm off. As for you (*to Simon*), when I come up to clean and clear you up, I'll bring him or her with me. You can keep an eye on it, dandle it on your lap. But that's all you'll get.

Simon Thank you.

Mandy So come along with you. You to your football, me to a snooze. And I suppose we'll have to go to the pub for our meal.

Simon Allow me – allow me to treat you. To the meal. At the pub. As it's partly my fault – (*hand goes into pocket, fishes out some money.*)

Greg Still, we can discuss a rise . . .

Mandy No we can't. Come on with you, I said.

Wood (*Erupts into the room, staring around wildly, with Simon's carrier bags.*) Where are they, where are – ? (*Sees them, drops Simon's carrier bags, goes to own with a moan of relief, checks contents.*)

Mandy These are ours, are they? (*Picks them up, hands them to Greg.*) There's lamb in there, chicken, butter, biscuits, cake – so we can eat at home after all.

Wood Yes, yes, all your filthy stuff. Killer foodstuff, animals slain, eggs pilfered – so guzzle, gobble, gobble, guzzle, cigarettes too, and you're pregnant.

Greg You don't speak to my Mandy like that, no you don't! (*Goes to Wood threateningly.*) I've seen inside your bags, I know what's in there. City trash is what you are! Look at you, trembling, shaking –

Mandy Home I said! (*Wheeling him out*) Home now. We've got everything we need. (*They go out.*)

Footsteps. Sound of car screeching, then driving sedately off.
Wood is standing, holding carrier bags at his chest, protectively.

Wood Missed your chance then. To dispose of the evidence.

Simon (*looking at him, after a pause*) Is that all you came back for?

Wood What else should I come back for?

Simon To see me. To put it right. All of it right. At last.

Wood It can never be put right. I learnt that much.

47

Simon Yes. Yes, it can. Look, stay with me here. Let me look after you. Be a good father to you at last.

Wood (*laughs*) I don't need a father any more. You're too late. Old man.

Simon Well then, just be my house guest. Come and go as you please. I'll keep you supplied with – with whatever I need. I promise.

Wood What you need I can get for myself. Until I don't need it any more.

> *Jeff enters. His clothes are in tatters. He is scratched, bruised, etcetera, slightly stunned.*

Simon Oh hello, Jeff. Here again. This – (*indicating Wood*) is my son.

Jeff (*ignoring Wood*) Hi. Can I have a drink? (*Lurches over to table, grabs bottle, opens it, swigs*) Aaagh! (*Looks at label.*) Port. Christ!

Wood (*to Simon, having flicked a contemptuous look at Jeff*) Well, that's you for a lifetime. That's what you are, da-da. A once in a lifetime experience.

Simon Wait! Where are you going, Jason? What will you do?

Wood (*Stares at him.*) Jason, Jason, the name's Julian, da-da. Julian Strapley. Son of the Wundale Wanker. (*Jabs two fingers at him, sticks out his tongue, goes.*)

Jeff (*taking this in, vaguely*) Didn't know you had a son. Thought you and Beth couldn't – or didn't want –

Simon He's not really my son. Just a – a – figure of speech, really. Well, (*taking Jeff in for first time*) what – how did you – ?

Jeff (*picking up another bottle*) Gin. More like it. (*Opens*

48

it, gulps.) Terrible business in the car. She wouldn't let go of the wheel, stamped on my foot on the accelerator, singing, shouting abuses, usual nightmare. Swerved into a fence, then while she was backing up, I threw myself out. Just in time. I don't think she even noticed – I could hear the sirens coming at her from all directions, a helicopter – she's for it this time. The slammer, a year or two at the least – and where does that leave me? Pootering up to jail during visiting hours? Unless she kills herself before they get her. (*Little pause.*) Poor Gwen. Poor old Gwen. I had to hitchhike back here, you know. A truck carrying fertilizer. Excuse the smell. (*Little pause.*) Didn't know what else to do. (*Gives a little laugh.*) Just like old times, eh, Simon?

Simon Yes. Yes, indeed. Old times. Look, Jeff, if you don't mind – there's a piece of music I was playing.

Jeff Fine. Fine by me. (*Pours himself a glug of gin, downs it, slams glass down on table, carries bottle to arm of sofa, sits down.*) Better than Plymouth, sober at a table, signing my frauds, eh? My babies – baby frauds. Poor, poor Gwen baby too.

Simon goes to CD equipment.

Jeff Oh, fuck! It's not 'Parsifal', is it? Please?

Simon 'Parsifal'?

Jeff You used to play it. All the time. My own fault. I introduced Wagner to you at Cambridge. But I couldn't take him now. Particularly haven't got the stamina for 'Parsifal' any more.

Simon Nor have I. No, this is the only thing I listen to these days. It's Beth, you see. Singing in the church choir. Just up the road. Ronnie – the vicar – made a recording a few years back. Thank God. She does a duet with – with um – the mother of my – my –

49

Jeff I didn't know Beth could sing.

Simon lets out a terrible howl of grief and rage.

Jeff (*Looks towards him, perplexed.*) You all right?

Simon Yes, fine, fine. She's a bit flat from time to time. But we won't mind that. Will we, Jeff?

Jeff Of course we won't. (*Raises bottle to lips.*) Of course not, Simon.

Simon turns switch. Church choir, Beth and Mandy singing their duet.
Simon sits, still and stiff, controlling himself. Jeff swigs contentedly from bottle as:

Curtain.